Study Smarter: Learn and Apply

Top 200 Drugs Pocketbook

- C-II
- Black Box Warning
- Drug Charts
- Abusive Drugs
- PRONOUNCIATION
- INDICATIONS

Pharmaduck

Thank You!

This guide is dedicated to anyone who wants to thrive and flourish their knowledge in the field of pharmacy. Whether you are scholar determined to earn a type of certificate, a doctorate degree, a grateful caregiver, or anyone at all, this pocket book will guide you through your classes in pharmacy school. Once again, thank you for your interest and investment in this guide, as this will set you forth to success, greatness, and step away from changing the world.

"And if you see me, smile and maybe give me a hug. That's important to me too."
- Jimmy V

"All that we see or seem is but a dream within a dream."
- Edgar Allen Poe

"Tell me, and I will forget. Show me, and I may remember. Involve me, and I will understand."
-Confucius

Dedicated to **Rex Thurgood** and all the students who are daring and dreaming to become great.

Terms of Use and Disclaimer

Notice of Liability, Privacy and Disclaimer: As the author of this eBook, I have made every effort to make the information in this book as accurate as possible. However, the information in the book is sold as is and without warranty. Pharmaduck are not liable for any damages caused directly or indirectly by the information in this book. Pharmaduck pledge to never make available to any third party your personal information. This book contains facts, views, opinions, statements, and recommendations of third party individuals, writers, advertisers, companies, and organizations. Pharmaduck books are for educational purposes only and should not be treated as medical advice. Nothing contained in this book is intended for medical diagnosis or treatment or substitute for consultation with a qualified healthcare professional. In no event will Pharmaduck, its partners, agents or contractors be liable for any damages or losses resulting from or caused by Pharmaduck and its services.

Let's Keep In Touch!

Reach out to us on social media. If you have any questions or concerns, please do not hesitate to reach us through the multiple social media platforms. (@Pharmaduck)

[Facebook](#)
[Twitter](#)
[LinkedIn](#)
[Google+](#)
[About Me](#)

Website:

http://pharmaduck.sitey.me/

Don't forget to join our mailing list!! We will send out free charts and continue to help develop brighter students that will care for the community, society, and the future of the world.

Mailing List:

http://eepurl.com/cWZruv

Copyright Notice:

All rights reserved. No part of this publication may be reproduced, distributed, or transmitted in any form or by any means, including photocopying, recording, or other electronic or mechanical methods, without the prior written permission of the publisher, except in the case of brief quotations embodied in critical reviews and certain other noncommercial uses permitted by copyright law.

Copyright © 2017 by **Pharmaduck**

Feedback:

Honest feedback and opinions are truly important in developing and building valuable material for students and future doctors. Please take your time and write us a review. The more reviews for our products, the faster we can produce updated versions free to the public.

Thank you again.

http://eepurl.com/cVqkYH

In addition to the pocketbooks to the public, we also have selected free e-books we would love to share with you in exchange for your interests in us!

These free e-books consists of drug charts, drug guidebooks, and leadership development guides.

Thank You!

Mission:

Ever felt that there are too many drugs to remember? Not only to remember, but to recall their generic names, brand names, indications, mechanism of actions, drug-drug interactions, and so… the list continues and continues and continues.

For me, when I was in pharmacy school, my professors tirelessly taught us complex concepts day after day after day, until we hit the "week", or better yet, the "night" before and cram all the scratches of notes, hour plus long podcast recordings, and dry powerpoint presentations for our midterm. Now, don't make me go into what happens during finals week and the aftermath of waiting to see your final grade after taking the final… we all we know how that feels…So let's not get into that.

Long story short, pharmacy school is a journey…some might call it a marathon (shout out to Prefontaine) and some might call it a quickie (shout out to Draymond). Nevertheless, these moments we spend in pharmacy school are the golden 20's or 30's or for some of us 40's…and these moments should be spent building covalent relationships with classmates, professors, and mentors.

After my years of doing what I love the most, I noticed that pharmacy students are capable of much more than they are taught in school. In this time of age, technology allows pharmacy students to look up medication information in a heartbeat. However, overtime students complain about feeling burnt out, anxious, depressed, and begin to bamboozle each other to compete for their life-long and successful career.

What has helped me, my mentees, friends and patients engrain pharmacy material effectively and efficiently is learning and understanding the concepts visually. Visual understanding and imagination presents great promises in achieving patient-centered care. The books, charts, and materials provided are here as a compass, to guide you to the right direction to strengthen your skills as a health care provider. Soar until you fly freely and understand visually.

-Pharmaduck

CHAPTER ONE
Top 200 Drug Charts

GENERIC	BRAND	INDICATION(S)
ANALGESICS/ANTI-INFLAMMATORY		
Acetaminophen (uh-see-tuh-min-uh-fuh n)	Tylenol Feverall	Non-Steroidal Anti-inflammatory/ Analgesic/ Antipyretic
Allopurinol (al-uh-pyoo r-uh-nawl)	Zyloprim	Gout Therapy
Aspirin (as-per-in)	Bayer Aspirin Ecotrin	Non-Steroidal Anti-inflammatory/ Anti-platelet
Buprenorphine Naloxone (bu-pri-nor-fin Nah-lox-one)	Suboxone (C-3)	Opioid Analgesic/ Opioid Antagonist Combinaiton
Celecoxib (Sel-eh-cox-ib)	Celebrex	Non-Steroidal Anti-inflammatory
Codeine/APAP 30/300mg (Co-dean)	Tylenol #3	Opioid Analgesic/ Analgesic Combinaiton
Fentanyl (Fen-tah-neal)	Duragesic (C-2)	Opioid Analgesic

Hydrocodone/APAP (Hi-droe-co-done)	Vicodin **(C-2)** Norco	Opioid Analgesic/ Analgesic Combinaiton
Hydromorphone (Hi-dro-morf-one)	Dilaudid	Opioid Analgesic
Ibuprofen (Eye-bu-pro-fin)	Motrin Advil	Non-Steroidal Anti-inflammatory
Ketorolac (Kit-or-oh-lack)	Toradol	Non-Steroidal Anti-inflammatory
Meloxicam (Mel-oxi-cam)	Mobic	Non-Steroidal Anti-inflammatory
Morphine (Morf-ean)	Ms Contin Ms IR	Opioid Analgesic
Naloxone (Nah-lox-one)	Narcan	Opioid Antagonist
Naproxen (Nah-prah-xen)	Aleve	Non-Steroidal Anti-inflammatory
Oxycodone (Ox-ee-co-done)	OxyContin **(C-2)**	Opioid Analgesic
Oxycodone/APAP (Ox-ee-co-done)	Percocet **(C-2)**	Opioid Analgesic/ Analgesic Combinaiton
Sumatriptan (Sooma-trip-tan)	Imitrex	Antimigraine/ Central Vasoconstrictor
Tramadol (Tram-ah-doll)	Ultram	Opioid Analgesic

ANTI-MICROBIAL

Acyclovir (Ah-cyclo-veer)	Zovirax	Antiviral
Amoxicillin (Aye-moxi-seal-in)	Amoxil Moxatag	Antibiotic
Amoxicillin/ Clavulanate (Clue-von-ate)	Augmentin	Antibiotic
Azithromycin (Ah-zi-throw-my-sin)	Zithromax Z-PAK	Antibiotic
Cefazolin (sef-ah-zo-lin)	Ancef	Antibiotic
Cefotaxime (sef-ah-tax-eam)	Claforan	Antibiotic
Ceftriaxone (sef-tree-ax-one)	Rocephin	Antibiotic
Cephalexin (sef-ah-lex-in)	Keflex Keftabs	Antibiotic
Ciprofloxacin (si-pro-flocks-ah-cin)	Cipro	Antibiotic
Clarithromycin (clah-rith-oh-my-sin)	Biaxin	Antibiotic
Clindamycin (clin-dah-my-sin)	Cleocin	Antibiotic
Doxycycline (docks-see-si-clean)	Vibramycin Doryx	Antibiotic
Fluconazole (flu-con-ah-zole)	Diflucan	Antifungal
Levofloxacin (le-vo-flox-ah-sin)	Levaquin	Antibiotic

Mupirocin (moo-peer-oh-sin)	Bactroban	Topical Antibiotic
Neomycin/Polymixin B/Bacitracin (nee-oh-my-sin) / (poll-ee-mix-in)/(back-tra-sin)	Neosporin Polysporin	Topical Antibiotic
Oseltamivir (oh-sel-tam-i-vir)	Tamiflu	Antiviral
Penicillin (pen-i-cill-in)		Antibiotic
Piperacillin/ Tazobactam (pip-er-ah-sil-in) / (tah-zoe-bact-um)	Zosyn	Antibiotic
Trimethoprim / Sulfamethoxazole (try-meth-oh-prim) / (sol-fah-meth-oxa-zole)	Bactrim Septra	Antibiotic
Terbinafine (tur-bean-ah-fine)	Lamasil	Topical Antifungal
Valacyclovir (val-ah-si-cyclo-vir)	Valtrex	Antiviral
Vancomycin (vank-oh-my-sin)	Vancocin	Antibiotic
AUTONOMIC		
Atropine (ah-tro-pin)	Atropen	Antimuscarinic

CARDIOVASCULAR

Amiodarone (amio-dare-one)	Cordarone Pacerone	Antiarrhythmic
Amlodipine (am-low-di-pean)	Norvasc	Antihypertensive
Amlodipine/ Atorvastatin (am-low-di-pean)	Caduet	Antihypertensive/ Hypolipemic
Amlodipine/ Benazepril (am-lo-di-pine)	Lotrel	Antihypertensive
Atenolol (ah-ten-oh-loll)	Tenormin	Antihypertensive
Atorvastatin (aye-tor-vah-stat-in)	Lipitor	Hypolipemic
Benazepril (beh-nahzeh-pril)	Lotensin	Antihypertensive
Carvedilol (carv-di-loll)	Coreg	Antihypertensive
Clonidine (cloney-din)	Catapres	Antihypertensive
Digoxin (dij-oxin)	Lanoxin Digitek	(inotrope) Antiarrhythmic
Dobutamine (dob-oo-tah-mean)	Dobutrex	Inotrope
Dopamine (dope-ahh-mean)	Dopastat Intropin	Inotrope/Pressor
Ezetimibe (ezet-i-mibe)	Zetia	Hypolipemic

Ezetimibe/ Simvastatin	Vytorin	Hypolipemic
Fenofibrate (feen-oh-figh-brate)	Tricor	Hypolipemic
Hydrochlorothiazide (hi-dro-chloro-thi-ah-zide)	Microzide	Diuretic/ HBP
Isosorbide Dinitrate (iso-or-bide)	Isordil	Antianginal
Isosorbide Mononitrate (isos-or-bide) (mawn-oh-i-trate)	Ismo Imdur	Antianginal
Lisinopril (ligh-sin-oh-pril)	Zestril Prinivil	Antihypertensive
Lisinopril/ Hydrochlorothiazide	Prinizide Zestoretic	Antihypertensive/ Diuretic Combination
Losartan (low-sar-tan)	Cozaar	Antihypertensive
Metoprolol succinate & tartrate (meh-top-pro-loll, suck-si-nate, tar-trate)	Toprol XL Loppressor	Antihypertensive
Nebivolol (neb-iv-oh-loll)	Bystolic	Antihypertensive
Nitroglycerin (nigh-tro-glis-er-in)	Nitrostat Nitrobid	Antianginal

Olmesartan (ohl-meh-sar-tan)	Benicar	Antihypertensive
Phenylephrine (fean-ahl-eff-frin)	Sudafed PE	Pressor/ Vasoconstrictor
Pravastatin (prah-vah-stat-in)	Pravachol	Hypolipemic
Rosuvastatin (roh-su-vah-statin)	Crestor	Hypolipemic
Sildenafil (sil-den-ah-fil)	Viagra	Vasodilator
Simvastatin (sim-vah-stat-in)	Zocor	Hypolipemic
Tadalafil (ta-dah-lah-fill)	Cialis	Vasodilator
Triamterene/ Hydrochlorothiazide (tree-am-tir-ean)	Maxide Diazide	Diuretic Combination
Valsartan (val-sarr-tan)	Diovan	Antihypertensive
Valsartan/ Hydrochlorothiazide	Diovan HCT	Antihypertensive/ Diuretic Combination
Verapamil (verr-ap-ahh-mil)	Calan Verelan	Antihypertensive/ Antiarrhythmic
Alprazolam (al-pra-zoe-lam)	Xanax **(C-4)**	Anxiolytics/ Sedatives/ Hypnotics

CENTRAL NERVOUS SYSTEM

Amitriptyline (am-ee-trip-tee-lean)	Elavil	Antidepressant
Amphetamine/ Dextroamphetamine (am-feta-mine), (dex-tro-am-fet-ah-mine)	Adderall XR **(C-2)**	Stimulant
Aripiprazole (ah-ri-prip-pra-zole)	Abilify	Antipsychotic
Bupropion (boo-pro-pee-on)	Wellbutrin	Antidepressant
Carisoprodol (carr-is-pro-doll)	Soma **(C-4)**	Skeletal Muscle Relaxant
Citalopram (sit-al-oh-pram)	Celexa	Antidepressant
Clonazepam (clo-nahz-a-pam)	Klonopin **(C-4)**	Anxiolytics/ Sedatives/ Hypnotics
Cyclobenzaprine (sigh-clo-benz-ah-prean)	Flexeril	Skeletal Muscle Relaxant
Desvenlafaxine (deh-sven-lah-fack-sin)	Pristiq	Antidepressant
Dexmethylphenidate (dex-meth-il-fen-i-date)	Focalin XR	Stimulant
Diazepam (di-ah-zi-pam)	Valium **(C-4)**	Anxiolytics/ Sedatives/ Hypnotics

Donepezil (doe-nep-ah-zil)	Aricept	Neurodegenerative Agent
Duloxetine (do-lox-ah-tean)	Cymbalta	Antidepressant
Escitalopram (eh-sight-al-lo-pram)	Lexapro	Anxiolytics/ Sedatives/ Hypnotics
Eszopiclone (es-zo-pic-lone)	Lunesta (C-4)	Anxiolytics/ Sedatives/ Hypnotics
Fluoxetine (flu-ox-eh-teen)	Proxac	Antidepressant
Gabapentin (gah-ba-pen-tin)	Neurontin	Anticonvulsant
Lidocaine (ligh-doe-cane)	Lidoderm Patch	Topical Anesthetic
Lidocaine	Xylocaine	Local-regional Anesthetic
Lisdexamfetamine (lis-decks-am-fet-ah-mean)	Vyvanse (C-2)	Stimulant
Lorazepam (lorr-ahz-ee-pam)	Ativan (C-4)	Anxiolytics/ Sedatives/ Hypnotics
Memantine (meh-man-teen)	Namenda	Neurodegenerative Agent
Methylphenidate ER (meth-el-fen-i-date)	Concerta (C-2)	Stimulant

Midazolam (mid-ah-zoe-lam)	Versed	Anxiolytics/ Sedatives/ Hypnotics
Olanzepine (oh-lanz-e-peen)	Zyprexa	Antipsychotic
Paroxetine (pah-rox-eh-teen)	Paxil	Antidepressant
Pregabalin (pre-gab-ah-lin)	Lyrica	Anticonvulsant
Promethazine (pro-meth-ah-zean)	Phenergan	Antitussive
Promethazine/ Codeine	Phenergan Codeine	Antitussive Combination
Propofol (pro-poe-fole)	Diprivan	General Anesthetic/ Sedative/Hypnotic
Quetiapine (quit-i-ahh-pin)	Seroquel Seroquel XR	Antipsychotic
Risperidone (risp-eri-done)	Risperdal	Antipsychotic
Sertraline (serr-trah-lean)	Zoloft	Antidepressant
Trazadone (trah-zah-done)	Desyrel	Antidepressant
Venlafaxine (ven-lahh-fack-sin)	Effexor	Antidepressant

Zolpidem (zole-pi-dem)	Ambien (C-4)	Anxiolytics/ Sedatives/ Hypnotics
Hydrocortisone (hi-dro-core-ti-sone)	Cortizone 10	Topical Corticosteroid
Triamcinolone (try-am-sin-i-lone)	Kenalog-40 Azmacort	Topical Corticosteroid

DERMATOLOGIC

Bismuth Subsalicylate (biz-muth, sub-sah-li-see-late)	Pepto Bismol Kaopectate	Acid/Peptic/ Gastric Anti-inflammatory

GASTROINTESTINAL

Docusate sodium (dock-que-sate)	Colace	Laxative
Esomeprazole (eh-so-me-prah-zall)	Nexium	Acid/Peptic/ Gastric Anti-inflammatory
Famotidine (fah-moe-tee-dean)	Pepcid AC	Acid/Peptic/ Gastric Anti-inflammatory
Lansoprazole (lans-oh-prah-zall)	Prevacid 24-Hour Prevacid	Acid/Peptic/ Gastric Anti-inflammatory
Omeprazole (oh-me-prah-zall)	Prilosec Prilosec OTC	Acid/Peptic/ Gastric Anti-inflammatory

Ondansetron (on-danh-se-trawn)	Zorfan	Antiemetic
Pantoprazole (pant-toe-prah-zall)	Protonix	Acid/Peptic/ Gastric Anti-inflammatory
Polyethylene Glycol 3350 (paul-ee-eth-ee-lean)	Miralax	Laxative
Prochlorperazine (pro-klor-perr-ah-zine)	Compazine	Antiemetic
Rabeprazole (ray-beh-prah-zall)	AcipHex	Acid/Peptic/ Gastric Anti-inflammatory
Ranitidine (rah-ni-ti-dean)	Zantac	Acid/Peptic/ Gastric Anti-inflammatory
Senna (sehh-nahh)	Senokot	Laxative
Clopidogrel (cloe-pih-doe-jrel)	Plavix	Anticoagulants
HEMATOLOGIC		
Dabigatran (daa-bee-gah-tran)	Pradaxa	Anticoagulants
Enoxaparin (ee-noxah-pah-rin)	Lovenox	Anticoagulants
Epoetin alpha (ee-poe-eh-tin, ah-l-fa)	Epogen Procrit	Growth factor

Ferrous Sulfate (feer-us, sul-fate)		Iron Preparation
Heparin (heh-parr-in)		Anticoagulants
Rivaroxaban (rivv-arr-ox-ah-ban)	Xarelto	Anticoagulants
Warfarin (warr-farr-in)	Coumadin	Anticoagulants
HORMONAL		
Conjugated Estrogens (con-juu-gate-ed)	Premarin	Female Sex Hormones
Dexamethasone (dex-ahh-meth-ahh-sone)	Decadron	Systemic Adrenal Corticosteroid
Dutasteride (du-tahh-sterr-ide)	Avodart	Antitestosterone
Ethinyl estradiol/ Drospirenone (eth-en-eel, est-rah-di-ole), (droe-spirr-eh-noone)	Yaz Yazmin	Contraceptive
Ethinyl estradiol/ Norethindrone (eth-in-eel, est-rah-di-ole) (norr-eth-in-drone)	Loestrin	Contraceptive

Etonogestrel/Ethinyl Estradiol (eh-to-no-geh-strell)	NuvaRing	Contraceptive
Glyburide (gly-burr-ide)	Micronase Diabeta	Antidiabetic
Hydrocortisone (hi-dro-core-ti-sone)	Solu-Cortef	Systemic Adrenal Corticosteroid
Insulin detemir (in-sull-in, deh-tee-mirr)	Levemir	Antidiabetic
Insulin glargine (glarr-gen)	Lantus Solostar	Antidiabetic
Insulin lispro (liss-pro)	Humalog	Antidiabetic
Insulin NPH (human)	Humulin N	Antidiabetic
Insulin Regular (human) (reg-u-larr)	Humulin R	Antidiabetic
Levothyroxine (lee-vo-thy-rox-een)	Synthyroid Levoxyl	Thyroid Agent
Metformin (mett-forr-men)	Glucophage	Antidiabetic
Methylprednisolone (meth-il-pred-ni-so-loan)	Medrol	Systemic Adrenal Corticosteroid
Pioglitazone (pee-oh-glit-ah-zone)	Actos	Antidiabetic

Prednisone (pred-ni-sone)	Deltasone	Systemic Adrenal Corticosteroid
Sitagliptin (sit-ag-lip-tin)	Januvia	Antidiabetic
Solifenacin (so-li-fen-ah-cin)	Vesicare	Nonvascular Smooth Muscle Relaxant

MISCELLANEOUS

Tamsulosin (tamm-su-low-sin)	Flomax	Nonvascular Smooth Muscle Relaxant
Tolterodine (toll-tear-oh-din)	Detrol LA	Nonvascular Smooth Muscle Relaxant
Latanoprost (lahh-ta-no-praust)	Xalantan	Topical Prostaglandin Analogue

OPTHALMIC

Alendronate (ah-len-dro-nate)	Fosamax	Bisphosphonate

RENAL/ELECTROLYTES

Calcitriol (cal-si-tri-ole)	Rocaltrol	Vitamin Derivative
Ergocalciferol (err-go-call-si-furr-ol)	Calciferol	Vitamin Derivative
Furosemide (furr-os-ehh-myde)	Lasix	Diuretic
Magnesium Sulfate (magg-nee-si-um)		Electrolyte

Potassium Chloride	Micro-K Slow-K	Electrolyte
Risedronate (rise-dro-nate)	Actonel	Bisphosphonate
Albuterol (al-bu-ter-oll)	Ventolin Proventil	Brochodilator
RESPIRATORY		
Beclomethasone (beck-lo-meth-ah-sone)	Qvar	Topical Corticosteroid
Budesonide (buu-deh-so-nide)	Rhinocort	Topical Corticosteroid
Budesonide/ Formoterol (for-mo-terr-ol)	Symbicort	Topical Corticosteroid/ Bronchodilator Combination
Cetirizine (cet-tri-zean)	Zyrtec	Anti-histamine
Dextromethorphan (dexx-tro-meth-orr-fan)		Anti-tussive
Diphenhydramine (di-fen-hi-dram-min)	Benadryl	Antihistamine
Fexofenadine	Allegra	Antihistamine
Fexofenadine/ Pseudoephedrine (fex-oh-fe-nahh-dine)	Allegra-D	Antihistamine/ Decongestant Combination
Fluticasone (flu-tic-ah-sone)	Flovent HFA Flonase	Topical Corticosteroid

Fluticasone/ Salmeterol (sal-meh-terr-oll)	Advair Diskus	Topical Corticosteroid/ Bronchodilator Combination
Guiafenesin (gu-ah-fen-ah-sin)	Robitussin Mucinex	Mucolytic
Ipratropium bromide (ip-ahh-tro-pium, bro-mide)	Atrovent	Brochodilator
Ipratropium bromide/ Albuterol (all-bu-terr-ol)	Combivent Respimat	Brochodilator Combinaiton
Levalbuterol (leh-vall-bu-terr-ole)	Xopenex	Brochodilator
Loratidine (lorr-ahh-ti-dean)	Claritin	Antihistamine
Loratidine/ Pseudoephedrine (lorr-ahh-ti-dean, suu-da-fe-drine)	Claritin-D 24Hour	Antihistamine/ Decongestant Combination
Mometasone (mo-meh-ta-sone)	Nasonex	Topical Corticosteroid
Montelukast (mon-tehh-luu-kast)	Singular	Immune Modulator
Pseudoephedrine (suu-do-fe-dren)	Sudafed	Decongestant

Tiotropium Bromide (ti-oe-tro-pi-um, bro-mide)	Spiriva HandiHaler	Brochodilator
Calcium Carbonate (cal-si-umm, carr-bon-ate)	Os-Cal	Vitamin Derivative
SUPPLEMENT		
Vitamin D3 (vi-ta-min)		Vitamin Derivative
VACCINE		
Vaccine - Influenza	Fluzone Fluarix Flumist	Vaccine (Viral)

Chapter Two

Scheduled Medications

Schedule I:	
Schedule I drugs, substances, or chemicals are defined as drugs with no currently accepted medical use and a high potential for abuse. Some examples of Schedule I drugs are:	
heroin	-
lysergic acid diethylamide	LSD
Marijuana	cannabis
3,4-methylenedioxymethamphetamine	ecstasy
methaqualone	-
peyote	-
Schedule II:	
Schedule II drugs, substances, or chemicals are defined as drugs with a high potential for abuse, with use potentially leading to severe psychological or physical dependence. These drugs are also considered dangerous. Some examples of Schedule II drugs are:	
Hydrocodone-acetaminophen	Vicodin, Norco
Cocaine	-
methamphetamine	-
Methadone	Methadose, Diskets, Dolophine
Meperidine	Demerol
oxycodone	OxyContin
fentanyl	Duragesics
Dexedrine	Dexedrine
Amphetamine / Dextroamphetamine	Adderall
methylphenidate	*Ritalin*
hydromorphone	*Dilaudid*

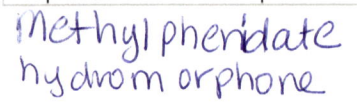

Methylphenidate	Ritalin
hydromorphone	Dilaudid

Schedule III:

Schedule III drugs, substances, or chemicals are defined as drugs with a moderate to low potential for physical and psychological dependence. Schedule III drugs abuse potential is less than Schedule I and Schedule II drugs but more than Schedule IV. Some examples of Schedule III drugs are:

hydromorphone	Dilaudid
Tylenol-codeine	Tylenol #3, Tylenol #4
ketamine	-
anabolic steroids	-
testosterone	-

Schedule IV:

Schedule IV drugs, substances, or chemicals are defined as drugs with a low potential for abuse and low risk of dependence. Some examples of Schedule IV drugs are:

Alprazolam	Xanax
Carisoprodol	Soma
Darvon	Darvon
Darvocet	Darvocet
Diazepam	Valium
Lorazepam	Ativan
Pentazocine	Talwin
Zolpidem	Ambien
Tramadol	Ryzolt, Ultram, ConZip

Schedule V:

Schedule V drugs, substances, or chemicals are defined as drugs with lower potential for abuse than Schedule IV and consist of preparations containing limited quantities of certain narcotics. Schedule V drugs are generally used for antidiarrheal, antitussive, and analgesic purposes. Some examples of Schedule V drugs are:

codeine and guaifenesin	Cheratussin AC
Atropine / Diphenoxylate	Lomotil
Atropine, difenoxin	Motofen
Pregabalin	Lyrica
Charcoal activated	Parepectolin

Let's Keep In Touch!

Reach out to us on social media. If you have any questions or concerns, please do not hesitate to reach us through the multiple social media platforms. (@Pharmaduck)

[Facebook](#)
[Twitter](#)
[LinkedIn](#)
[Google+](#)
[About Me](#)

Website: @ http://pharmaduck.sitey.me/

Pharmaduck
Pharmaceuticals

Don't forget to join our mailing list!! We will send out free charts and continue to help develop brighter students that will care for the community, society, and the future of the world.

Mailing List: @ http://eepurl.com/cVqkYH

Free E-Book: @ http://eepurl.com/cVqkYH

In addition to the pocketbooks to the public, we also have selected free e-books we would love to share with you in exchange for your interests in us!

These free e-books consists of drug charts, drug guidebooks, and leadership development guides.

Thank You!

Chapter Three

Drug Addiction Treatments

Principles of Drug Addiction Treatment

More than three decades of scientific research show that treatment can help drug-addicted individuals stop drug use, avoid relapse and successfully recover their lives. Based on this research, 13 fundamental principles that characterize effective drug abuse treatment have been developed. These principles are detailed in NIDA's Principles of Drug Addiction Treatment: A Research-Based Guide. The guide also describes different types of science-based treatments and provides answers to commonly asked questions.

1. Addiction is a complex but treatable disease that affects brain function and behavior. Drugs alter the brain's structure and how it functions, resulting in changes that persist long after drug use has ceased. This may help explain why abusers are at risk for relapse even after long periods of abstinence.

2. No single treatment is appropriate for everyone. Matching treatment settings, interventions, and services to an individual's particular problems and needs is critical to his or her ultimate success.

3. Treatment needs to be readily available. Because drug-addicted individuals may be uncertain about entering treatment, taking advantage of available services the moment people are ready for treatment is critical. Potential patients can be lost if treatment is not immediately available or readily accessible.

4. Effective treatment attends to multiple needs of the individual, not just his or her drug abuse. To be effective, treatment must address the individual's drug

abuse and any associated medical, psychological, social, vocational, and legal problems.

5. Remaining in treatment for an adequate period of time is critical. The appropriate duration for an individual depends on the type and degree of his or her problems and needs. Research indicates that most addicted individuals need at least 3 months in treatment to significantly reduce or stop their drug use and that the best outcomes occur with longer durations of treatment.

6. Counseling—individual and/or group—and other behavioral therapies are the most commonly used forms of drug abuse treatment. Behavioral therapies vary in their focus and may involve addressing a patient's motivations to change, building skills to resist drug use, replacing drug-using activities with constructive and rewarding activities, improving problemsolving skills, and facilitating better interpersonal relationships.

7. Medications are an important element of treatment for many patients, especially when combined with counseling and other behavioral therapies. For example, methadone and buprenorphine are effective in helping individuals addicted to heroin or other opioids stabilize their lives and reduce their illicit drug use. Also, for persons addicted to nicotine, a nicotine replacement product (nicotine patches or gum) or an oral medication (buprorion or varenicline), can be an effective component of treatment when part of a comprehensive behavioral treatment program.

8. An individual's treatment and services plan must be assessed continually and modified as necessary to ensure it meets his or her changing needs. A patient may require varying combinations of services and treatment components during the course of treatment and recovery. In addition to counseling or psychotherapy, a patient may

This chart may be reprinted. Citation of the source is appreciated.

require medication, medical services, family therapy, parenting instruction, vocational rehabilitation and/or social and legal services. For many patients, a continuing care approach provides the best results, with treatment intensity varying according to a person's changing needs.

9. Many drug-addicted individuals also have other mental disorders. Because drug abuse and addiction—both of which are mental disorders—often co-occur with other mental illnesses, patients presenting with one condition should be assessed for the other(s). And when these problems co-occur, treatment should address both (or all), including the use of medications as appropriate.

10. Medically assisted detoxification is only the first stage of addiction treatment and by itself does little to change long-term drug abuse. Although medically assisted detoxification can safely manage the acute physical symptoms of withdrawal, detoxification alone is rarely sufficient to help addicted individuals achieve long-term abstinence. Thus, patients should be encouraged to continue drug treatment following detoxification.

11. Treatment does not need to be voluntary to be effective. Sanctions or enticements from family, employment settings, and/or the criminal justice system can significantly increase treatment entry, retention rates, and the ultimate success of drug treatment interventions.

12. Drug use during treatment must be monitored continuously, as lapses during treatment do occur. Knowing their drug use is being monitored can be a powerful incentive for patients and can help them withstand urges to use drugs. Monitoring also provides an early indication of a return to drug use, signaling a possible

need to adjust an individual's treatment plan to better meet his or her needs.

13. Treatment programs should assess patients for the presence of HIV/AIDS, hepatitis B and C, tuberculosis, and other infectious diseases, as well as provide targeted risk-reduction counseling to help patients modify or change behaviors that place them at risk of contracting or spreading infectious diseases. Targeted counseling specifically focused on reducing infectious disease risk can help patients further reduce or avoid substance-related and other high-risk behaviors. Treatment providers should encourage and support HIV screening and inform patients that highly active antiretroviral therapy (HAART) has proven effective in combating HIV, including among drug-abusing populations.

Chapter Four

List of Controlled Medications

List of Common Controlled Medications

Actiq®	Dexedrine®
Adderall®	Dextroamphetamine
Alfenta®	Dextrostat®
Alfentanil	Diazepam
Alprazolam	Diazepam®
Alzapam®	Dilaudid®
Ambien®	Dilaudid-HP®
Anexsia®	Dolacet®
Anodynos-DHC®	Dolophine®
Astramorph®	Dover's Powder®
Ativan®	Duadyne DHC®
Attenta®	Duocet®
Azdone®	Duragesic®
Benzedrine	Duramorph®
Beta-phenyl-isopropylamine	E-Lor®
Buprenex®	Empirin® with Codeine
Buprenorphine	Endocet®
Butorphanol	Epimorph®
Carisoprodol	Equasym®
Chlorazepate	Estazolam
Chlordiazepoxide	Fentanyl
Choral Hydrate	Fentanyl®
Clonazepam	Ferndex®

Cocaine	Fiorinal® with Codeine
Cocaine® Topical Solution	Flunitrazepam
Codeine	Flurazepam
Codoxyn®	Focalin®
Co-Gesic®	Genagesic®
Concerta®	Halcion®
Dalmane®	Hydrocet®
Damason-P®	Hydrocodone
Darvocet-N®	Hydromorphone
Darvon®	Hydrostat IR®
Darvon-N®	Hy-Phen®
Daytrana®	Infumorph®
Demerol®	Klonopin®
Desoxyephedrine	Levo-Dromoran®
Levorphanol	ProSom®
Librium®	Resoxyn®
Lorax®	Restoril®
Lorazepam	Ritalin®
Lorcet®	Ritalina®
Lortab®	Ritaline®
Lunesta®	RMS®
Mepergan®	Rohypnol®
Meperidine	Roxanol®
Metadate®	Roxanol-SR®
Methadone	Roxicet®
Methamphetamine	Roxicodone®
Methylin®	Roxilox®
Methylphenidate	Roxiprin®
Methylphenidate	Rubifen®

Morphine	Secobarbital
Morphine Sulfate®	Seconal®
MS Contin®	Serax®
MSIR®	Soma®
Noctec®	Stadol®
Norcet®	Statex®
Norco®	Sublimaze®
Novosecobarb®	Temazepam
Opium	Tranxene®
Opium Tincture®	Triazolam
Oralet®	Tylenol® with Codeine
Oramorph SR®	Tylox®
Oxazepam	Uniserts®
Oxycet®	Valium®
Oxycodone	Valrelease®
OxyContin®	Vicodin®
OxyFAST®	Vicoprofen®
OxyIR®	Wygesic®
Percocet®	Xanax®
Percodan-Demi®	Zetran®
Propacet®	Zydone®
Propoxyphene	

CHAPTER FIVE
Abusive Drugs

Most drugs of abuse can alter a person's thinking and judgment, leading to health risks, including addiction, drugged driving and infectious disease. Most drugs could potentially harm an unborn baby; pregnancy-related issues are listed in the chart below for drugs where there is enough scientific evidence to connect the drug use to specific negative effects

- Alcohol
- Ayahuasca
- Cocaine
- DMT
- GHB
- Hallucinogens
- Heroin
- Inhalants
- Ketamine
- Khat
- Kratom
- LSD
- Marijuana (Cannabis)
- MDMA (Ecstasy/Molly)
- Mescaline (Peyote)
- Methamphetamine
- Over-the-counter Cough/Cold Medicines (Dextromethorphan or DXM)
- PCP
- Prescription Opioids
- Prescription Sedatives (Tranquilizers, Depressants)
- Prescription Stimulants
- Psilocybin
- Rohypnol® (Flunitrazepam)
- Salvia
- Steroids (Anabolic)
- Synthetic Cannabinoids
- Synthetic Cathinones (Bath Salts)

Let's Keep In Touch!

Reach out to us on social media. If you have any questions or concerns, please do not hesitate to reach us through the multiple social media platforms. (@Pharmaduck)

[Facebook](#)
[Twitter](#)
[LinkedIn](#)
[Google+](#)
[About Me](#)

Website: @ http://pharmaduck.sitey.me/

Pharmaduck
Pharmaceuticals

Don't forget to join our mailing list!! We will send out free charts and continue to help develop brighter students that will care for the community, society, and the future of the world.

Mailing List: @ http://eepurl.com/cVqkYH

Pharmaduck Mailing List

Free E-Book: @ http://eepurl.com/cVqkYH

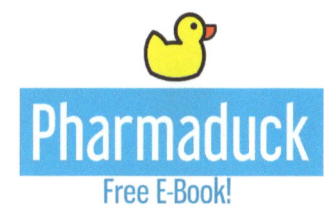

Pharmaduck Free E-Book!

In addition to the pocketbooks to the public, we also have selected free e-books we would love to share with you in exchange for your interests in us!

These free e-books consists of drug charts, drug guidebooks, and leadership development guides.

Thank You!

CPSIA information can be obtained
at www.ICGtesting.com
Printed in the USA
LVHW072130090419
613585LV00015B/514/P